A Conversation With My

Adult Children

FGA COIDO

Contents

Dedication

To my parents for the anchoring, freedom, and empowerment you gave me.

To my brother, my guardian angel, my rock, the wise man and the eldest.

To my children, who are a source of love every day.

Finally, she is the pillar, my wife—thank you. I am myself every day because of you.

Acknowledgments

To my friends and colleagues, for your constant support, encouragement, and the expectation for me to do better every day.

About the Author

I am a husband, a dad, a son and a brother first. My journey is multifaceted. Influenced by notable thinkers like Fanon, Césaire, Camus, and Saint-Exupéry, my background has shaped my strong sense of identity and social values. From Paris to London as my anchors and my travels as exploration tool of self-discovery I have developed a strong sense of identity, which growth and develop further after each encounter and reflective practice.

The process was simple. It was about my thought in the early hours of the day.

I will write them on a board and hang them in the kitchen, take a picture and send them to the family WhatsApp group.

January

"Define and/or review your goals in a timely manner; being short, medium, or long term."

Notes

Action

"Be ready for life. Start with today. Start with a smile (it tricks your brain into thinking you're happy, and it works as it releases Dopamine)."

Notes

Action

"For something to happen, you have to make it happen!"

Notes

Action

"Be aware of your surroundings, your needs, and strategies to avoid the glaring pitfalls on your way to success."

Notes

Action

"Be out there. Don't hide. Walk proudly on the successful path."

Notes

Action

"In adversity, you will discover the true warrior within."

Notes

Action

"When you feel rushed, don't panic. Just expand the time. Breathe through it."

Notes

Action

"Listen to your body. This is the vehicle of your exploits. Listen to your instinct. This is the driver and the map reader. Listen to the universe, and you will discover the map."

Notes

Action

"Who do you believe in?"

Notes

Action

"Be very clear and direct when speaking. Tell people what you need from them."

Notes

Action

"Don't be afraid to take action. Don't be afraid of the unknown. Don't live afraid."

Notes

Action

"You need to look forward to finding your way."

Notes

Action

"There are no 'safe' ways to success."

Notes

Action

"Be responsible for your actions. Take ownership of
your decisions. Accept your choices."

Notes

Action

"Don't wait to fix a problem, as it will only make it more complex."

Notes

Action

"Enjoy other people's company and tell them."

Notes

Action

"When you think about it, you have the answers to
most of your questions. Just remove the veil!"

Notes

Action

"If you want to run effectively, you need to maintain your form. Look straight ahead, use short strides, and take small steps. Think about your way to success, now."

Notes

Action

"Take the time to grow. Respect the cycle of the universal laws."

Notes

Action

"Be brave and face your future. No matter how uncertain it seems."

Notes

Action

February

"Create the environment to be your best."

Notes

Action

"Avoid a false start by being disciplined, vigilant, and focused on the end game."

Notes

Action

"Make sure you remove from your body any foreign objects, look after your cuts, and don't over-exhaust it too often."

Notes

Action

"Now it's about relaunching!"

Notes

Action

"Learn to say 'No'."

Notes

Action

"Keep focus on the task, stay on course. Ignore the noise around, even the whispers. Just be prepared for anything. But most of all, be yourself at all times."

Notes

Action

"Don't force your way in. Doors will open when you are ready."

Notes

Action

"When a door closes, another one opens. Just be
prepared to walk through the threshold."

Notes

Action

"Give the solution time to be effective."

Notes

.

Action

"Don't hesitate to make connections with people, places, and ideas."

Notes

Action

"Don't let the past dictate the future!"

Notes

Action

"Don't let the noise around you distract you. Keep focus on your journey."

Notes

Action

"You know you're home when you feel happy just by being there!"

Notes

Action

"You know when something has run its course. Be decisive and move on!"

Notes

Action

"Make sure to express your sadness, your joy, and happiness, as this is the fuel that will propel you forward."

Notes

Action

March

"To complete the course, you need to visualize past the finishing line."

Notes

Action

"Don't forget to socialise. A great night could be good food and fantastic people!"

Notes

Action

"Make sure you connect to people. Don't isolate yourself too much, as you will miss the beauty of the whole."

Notes

Action

"Be assertive, not aggressive. Just say what needs to be said, just do what needs to be done, do it with love."

Notes

Action

"To become an expert always starts with the basics.
They are the foundations of knowledge."

Notes

Action

"When you've reached your destination, take it in and keep going, as nothing stops in the universe."

Notes

Action

"Just say enough about what you do, for people not to be negative about it and slow down your progress."

Notes

Action

"When carrying a plan, don't waiver, just stay on course until the end. Don't let emotions derail the journey!"

Notes

Action

"Certain choices are difficult but necessary. As long as they are just and fair, one must make them."

Notes

Action

"To progress smoothly, you will need to be able to read people. Trust your instinct."

Notes

Action

"After reflection and planning, actions are needed to achieve one's goal."

Notes

Action

"Physical and intellectual inactivity literally kill us!"

Notes

Action

"Meditate, have you taken the time to meditate? Do it daily, and it will help you to see more clearly!"

Notes

Action

"Don't crumble under pressure. Just start by putting one foot forward. Start with the basics."

Notes

Action

"By visualizing it, you can see your future."

Notes

Action

"Establishing a routine is the best way to achieve your goals."

Notes

Action

"Create a safe and tidy environment to improve your well-being, mentally, emotionally, and physically."

Notes

Action

April

"To complete the course, you need to visualize past the finishing line."

Notes

Action

"Don't forget to socialise. A great night could be good food and fantastic people!"

Notes

Action

"Make sure you connect to people. Don't isolate yourself too much, as you will miss the beauty of the whole."

Notes

Action

"Be assertive, not aggressive. Just say what needs to be said, just do what needs to be done, do it with love."

Notes

Action

"To become an expert always starts with the basics.
They are the foundations of knowledge."

Notes

Action

"When you've reached your destination, take it in and keep going, as nothing stops in the universe."

Notes

Action

"Just say enough about what you do, for people not to be negative about it and slow down your progress."

Notes

Action

"When carrying a plan, don't waiver, just stay on course until the end. Don't let emotions derail the journey!"

Notes

Action

"Certain choices are difficult but necessary. As long as they are just and fair, one must make them."

Notes

Action

"To progress smoothly, you will need to be able to read people. Trust your instinct."

Notes

Action

"After reflection and planning, actions are needed to achieve one's goal."

Notes

Action

"Physical and intellectual inactivity literally kill us!"

Notes

Action

"Meditate, have you taken the time to meditate? Do it daily, and it will help you to see more clearly!"

Notes

Action

"Don't crumble under pressure. Just start by putting one foot forward. Start with the basics."

Notes

Action

"By visualizing it, you can see your future."

Notes

Action

"Establishing a routine is the best way to achieve your goals."

Notes

Action

"Create a safe and tidy environment to improve your well-being, mentally, emotionally, and physically."

Notes

Action

May

"Don't let the past hold you down. Engage with the
present and create your future."

Notes

Action

"All our thoughts have an impact. All our talks have an impact. All our actions have an impact. We create our future."

Notes

Action

"Be your own judge. Don't be too harsh; just be fair. Then, move with the expectation that you learn. If not… start again."

Notes

Action

"What do you hear? When someone says: 'The work starts now!' Consistency, teamwork, team ethics, hard work, resilience, intellectual commitment, decision process, decision making, emotional well-being."

Notes

Action

"Remember, not to be surprised by others' reactions. What you see as normal is extraordinary in their eyes and vice versa."

Notes

Action

"Don't let the flow of life take you unconsciously, as you can always steer your boat in the right direction. Sometimes, the course is correct; other times, it needs correction. 'Straightforward, left, right, but consider U-turn too.'"

Notes

Action

"Excellence is excellence. You are more likely to achieve it if you can see it, touch it, feel it, and breathe it. Don't hesitate to learn from others or nature to reach your goal."

Notes

Action

"Pace yourself by listening to the world around you, by feeling the wind, the rain, or the warmth of the sun on your skin. Pace yourself by feeling the space and time around you!"

Notes

Action

"Feed your mind as you're feeding your body. To diet successfully, you need a goal. When you reach it, now the work starts."

Notes

Action

"Nothing like going for a walk or being outside to start a fulfilling day!"

Notes

Action

"Superpowers! In the morning, breathe thoroughly barefoot while taking in the morning light! Rise early and breathe."

Notes

Action

"Don't force yourself into a diet. Instead, learn to know what nourishes your body and makes you happy. Be disciplined and as adventurous as you like! But remember, every action has a consequence."

Notes

Action

"You will meet the people you need to meet at the right time in your life. Learn, exchange, grow with them, but make sure you keep your direction of travel."

Notes

Action

"Sometimes, just take a break and observe life around you!"

Notes

Action

"To stay 'alive,' make connections with people, nature, and your inner self. Being 'alive' is being your true self; it's being your whole self."

Notes

Action

"Don't let the past dictate the future!"

Notes

Action

"Don't let the noise around you distract you. Keep focus on your journey."

Notes

Action

"You know you're home when you feel happy just
by being there!"

Notes

Action

"You know when something has run its course. Be decisive and move on!"

Notes

Action

"Make sure to express your sadness, your joy, and happiness, as this is the fuel that will propel you forward."

Notes

Action

"Don't forget to socialise. A great night could be good food and fantastic people!"

Notes

Action

"To finish in a good time, you need to visualize past the finishing line."

Notes

Action

"Just say enough about what you do, for people not to be negative about it and slow down your progress."

Notes

Action

"When you've reached your destination, take it in and keep going, as nothing stops in the universe."

Notes

Action

"Certain choices are difficult but necessary. As long as they are just and fair, one must make them."

Notes

Action

"When carrying a plan, don't waiver, just stay on course until the end. Don't let emotions derail the journey!"

Notes

Action

"By visualizing it, you can see your future."

Notes

Action

"Establishing a routine is the best way to achieve your goals."

Notes

Action

"Create a safe and tidy environment to improve your well-being, mentally, emotionally, and physically."

Notes

Action

June

"Trick your brain into happiness by smiling.
Smiling helps you focus on positive outcomes."

Notes

Action

"Boredom enhances creativity and well-being. We should embrace our mind's need to wander."

Notes

Action

"Well-planned small steps are the shortest way to
your goal."

Notes

Action

"Learn to know what you don't know. Learn to do what you can't do. If you want to be successful."

Notes

Action

"Take your time to meditate daily. Don't force it, and it will become one of the pillars of your success."

Notes

Action

"Appreciate the little things in life. They often have the greatest impact."

Notes

Action

"Growth begins where comfort ends. Step out of your comfort zone."

Notes

Action

"Success is not final, failure is not fatal: It is the courage to continue that counts."

Notes

Action

"The best preparation for tomorrow is doing your best today."

Notes

Action

"Embrace challenges as opportunities to grow stronger and wiser."

Notes

Action

"When in doubt, follow your instinct and smile."

Notes

Action

"You carry the keys of your happiness. Unlock the padlock to success by following your dreams."

Notes

Action

"Don't let anger take over as you do not express your emotions. Talk, sing, dance, write, draw, and play to express your feelings. Any feeling. The time and place will come to you intuitively."

Notes

Action

"Create the space and allocate the time to find your inner peace. Don't let anything or anyone take over your space and waste your time unless you've agreed by prior consent."

Notes

Action

"Project your dreams. See them, verbalize them, and write them down for your eyes only. You have to trust the universe's laws; you have to trust yourself. Have faith."

Notes

Action

"When you recognize a lack of skills, the daily discipline of personal growth will start to make things happen. Develop your personal growth journey → Discipline and routine are a start."

Notes

Action

"If you think people, you attract could be better,
then it's time for you to improve yourself."

Notes

Action

"Stand still. Stand still during the day. Shut out the noise. Take time to pause. Take time to reflect. Take time to recharge. Just be present. Just take time to be."

Notes

Action

"The best plan of battle should not be talked about. Formalize them, and write them down. Only reveal to allies what they need to know. Keep the full picture to yourself and your inner circle."

Notes

Action

July

"Carpe diem – seize the day!"

Notes

Action

"Enjoy the day. Start with a smile."

Notes

Action

"Enjoy the day! Start with a plan. Start with your plan."

Notes

Action

"Enjoy the day! Don't compromise your principles, but adjust the course of action to stay on your path of success."

Notes

Action

"Enjoy the day! Don't overthink it. Let the flow carry you!"

Notes

Action

"Enjoy the day! Make the most of it! Make the best of it!"

Notes

Action

"Enjoy the day! Be clear about your direction of travel and keep the course. Believe in your destination, as you can accomplish everything you set your mind to."

Notes

Action

"Enjoy the day! Just let go and take it in!"

Notes

Action

"You succeed at what you are prepared to see. You see what you are prepared to see. → Visualization."

Notes

Action

"When in doubt, follow your instinct and smile."

Notes

Action

"Jettison the judgement. Get rid of unwanted
language, thoughts, people."

Notes

Action

"Visualize yourself in the action you want to perform."

Notes

Action

"The strongest of all warriors are the two: Time and Patience."

Notes

Action

"Good things come to those who wait."

Notes

Action

"Patience is not the ability to wait, but the ability to keep a good/positive attitude while waiting."

Notes

Action

"Positive failure is failure after appropriate investment that leads to further learning, development, and growth. Precondition for positive failure: Acceptance of one's own vulnerability. Having a growth mindset. Embracing imperfection."

Notes

Action

"Don't forget your plan. Read it daily if you need to. Remember, it needs to be written down to materialize."

Notes

Action

"Define a space and a time to read your plan. Create a routine."

Notes

Action

"Wake up early at the same time every day."

Notes

Action

"Balance health, body, and soul. Create a physical activity routine as you are doing for everything."

Notes

Action

August

"Reflect and look in the mirror. Accept your own vulnerability. Don't be scared, it's a strength."

Notes

Action

"Improve your mindset – by believing that your abilities are not innate but can be improved through effort, learning, and persistence. Developing a growth mindset is the attitude when facing challenges."

Notes

Action

"You need to accept yourself with all your imperfections. They will humanize you and draw people to you. The right people."

Notes

Action

"Breathe. Take time to breathe."

Notes

Action

"Breathe. Using breathing to define time: Slow it...
Stop it... Extend it..."

Notes

Action

"Breathe. Start a daily routine. Create a ritual."

Notes

Action

"Be active. To find balance in life: Be active mentally. Be active physically. Be active socially."

Notes

Action

"Sleep: to restore, to grow, and to guide you. Sleeping is the key. Develop a pattern to optimize its power."

Notes

Action

"Sleep. Develop a routine and stick to it. Create an uncluttered space to create an uncluttered mind."

Notes

Action

"With patience comes great reward.'Patience is bitter, but its fruit is sweet (J.J. Rousseau)."

Notes

Action

"Be present at all times. Go with the flow."

Notes

Action

"We limit ourselves when we are judging others."

Notes

Action

"'You are never too old to set another goal or to dream a new dream.' (C.S. Lewis)"

Notes

Action

"Expect the best to achieve your best. Be ready to receive the gifts of life, the universal law."

Notes

Action

"Be physically, mentally, spiritually, financially, socially, and morally ready to achieve your best. Plan, train, review, and start again."

Notes

Action

"Create your future by designing your own path."

Notes

Action

"When drawing up your plan, be honest and realistic. Don't deceive yourself; nothing is easy."

Notes

Action

"Be open to the gifts of life."

Notes

Action

"Think less, act more. Do without knowing why?
Trust yourself."

Notes

Action

"Follow your instinct. Don't question it. Just trust and don't procrastinate."

Notes

Action

"To unburden your mind, create a special space,
physically and mentally."

Notes

Action

"Active listening doesn't always need verbal feedback, it needs acknowledgement."

Notes

Action

"To see the 'invisible,' be ready to see the unexpected. Grow a mindset able to receive new information."

Notes

Action

"Appreciate the moment by fully living, being present in that time and space. Just let it flow."

Notes

Action

"When was the last time you took time to breathe?"

Notes

Action

"Sometimes others will see you as you are. Accept it."

Notes

Action

"Be prepared to accept another point of view. It's not a 'judgement,' just another interpretation."

Notes

Action

"Be prepared to save time later."

Notes

Action

"The people we come across on our journey are there for a reason. Being self-reflective mirrors, foes, companions, or guides."

Notes

Action

"Live fully in the present. Don't overthink it, live a life of action."

Notes

Action

"Be yourself. Don't pretend to be who you are not! Accept yourself as you are. That is the way to grow."

Notes

Action

"When you make a decision, stick to it. Even if the path is not clear, follow your instinct."

Notes

Action

"Take time to breathe during the day. It's the best to recharge your body, mind, and soul."

Notes

Action

"Follow the flow. Follow your dream. Never underestimate what you are capable of."

Notes

Action

"Better a limited circle of friends than a lot of timewasters. Be aware of the 'butterfly.' Be social but on your own terms."

Notes

Action

"Let opportunities come to you. Choose the one that appeals to all your senses, your instinct, and commit fully."

Notes

Action

"Don't let opportunities pass you by due to fear of failure."

Notes

Action

"Keep things simple, and they will materialize."

Notes

Action

"Recognise your guide by their familiarity. Don't be afraid of the other, but embrace their differences."

Notes

Action

"Never underestimate others: friends, foes, and everything in between."

Notes

Action

"Timing is everything. Don't overstretch if you want to reach your goal and keep going."

Notes

Action

"To steer the ship in the right direction, check its course regularly."

Notes

Action

"Having those difficult conversations is the only way forward on a growth path."

Notes

Action

"Improve your well-being, and the one of the people you meet, by showing gratitude. It's simple! Start with thank you!"

Notes

Action

"To improve your well-being and capacity to see the road ahead, make sure you respect your sleep and downtime."

Notes

Action

"Pacing oneself with a realistic beginning and ending time will enable anyone to achieve their goals."

Notes

Action

"To achieve your full potential, you must love life in all its forms. You must love yourself with all your strengths and weaknesses."

Notes

Action

"To accept the path you are on, you need to accept that it's the result of your choices. To change a path, it's about changing yourself. Start with true universal love!"

Notes

Action

"Don't be distracted by other people's behaviour.

Notes

Action

September

"Recognize your guide by his/her familiarity. Don't be afraid of the other, but embrace their differences."

Notes

Action

"Never underestimate others: friends, foes, and everything in between."

Notes

Action

"Timing is everything. Don't overstretch if you want to reach your goal and keep going."

Notes

Action

"To steer the ship in the right direction, check its course regularly."

Notes

Action

"Having those difficult conversations is the only way forward on a growth path."

Notes

Action

"Improve your well-being, and the one of the people you meet, by showing gratitude. It's simple! Start with thank you!"

Notes

Action

"To improve your well-being and capacity to see the road ahead; make sure you respect your sleep and downtime."

Notes

Action

"Pacing oneself with a realistic beginning and ending time will enable anyone to achieve their goals."

Notes

Action

"To achieve your full potential, you must love life in all its forms. You must love yourself with all your strengths and weaknesses."

Notes

Action

"To accept the path you are on, you need to accept that it's the result of your choices. To change a path, it's about changing yourself. Start with true universal love!"

Notes

Action

"Don't be distracted by other people's behaviour.
Follow your plan and keep the focus on your goal."

Notes

Action

"It's important to express your feelings, emotions, and thoughts in the right place to the right people at the right time if possible. Don't fear being judged; these are your feelings, emotions, and thoughts. Alternatively, you can pray or meditate."

Notes

Action

"Sometimes just sleeping is the answer to the ills of the body."

Notes

Action

"Never underestimate the value of hard work, patience, and intuition."

Notes

Action

"Always give the best of yourself even when at your lowest. Give what you have, not what people expect, but give willingly."

Notes

Action

"When you are ready to do something: Write it down and make sure you have a timeline."

Notes

Action

"If you wait to make a decision, the opportunity will be gone! Don't rush it by being emotional. Just proceed when ready."

Notes

Action

"Go about your business with no fear, feeling of revenge or resentment. Just do what needs to be done, say what needs to be said in order to clear the path of success."

Notes

Action

"If you want it done; start the process. Have a clear plan and start by yourself."

Notes

Action

"Express your feelings in any way you want and move on to the successful path. Move on to a fulfilling life."

Notes

Action

October

"Respect the flow of life with its wrong turns, twisted paths, and dead ends, as they forced you to reflect and adjust to stay on the successful healthy path."

Notes

Action

"You must be honest with yourself as reality will bring you back to earth."

Notes

Action

"When you have to make a decision, no one can do it for you!"

Notes

Action

"Be real! Acting up always catches up with you."

Notes

Action

"Use memories to boost your future, not to drag you back."

Notes

Action

"Assumption is the mother of all mistakes as the lowest form of knowledge."

Notes

Action

"Don't try to stop the inevitable, as you will just delay or postpone it at best."

Notes

Action

"Practise Ubuntu daily by forgiving others, by acknowledging their humanity. Ubuntu → being self through others."

Notes

Action

"Create a weekly structure. Define your character.
Review weekly."

Notes

Action

"To be successful, structure your week, create a motto, and create your future."

Notes

Action

"Look at yourself and develop your skills and character daily."

Notes

Action

"When you hit a wall, find a way to get back on your feet and carry out the mission."

Notes

Action

"Don't fear the unknown, but embrace it!"

Notes

Action

"Embrace life totally. Be ambitious. Be positive. Be authentic."

Notes

Action

"Embrace everything you do with: Courage, Humility, Discipline."

Notes

Action

"Evolution, improvement, success. Change one thing at a time and stick to it until you learn."

Notes

Action

"What is your 'Motto'? It must be 3 statements, 3 lines, or 3 words. Rule of three applies!"

Notes

Action

"My Motto is: Success with humility. Success with humanity. Success with communities."

Notes

Action

"No one can make a decision for you. Take it, and don't think about it anymore!"

Notes

Action

"It's not about being nice, but about being oneself."

Notes

Action

November

"Learn, Learn, Learn. Challenge yourself and learn new skills – Anytime, Any day, Any place."

Notes

Action

"Adapt, as today's truth is not tomorrow's reality."

Notes

Action

"Accept who you are with your strengths and weaknesses. Decide who you want to be. Decide how you want to get there. Decide on your journey."

Notes

Action

"Invest in yourself. Discover new horizons, learn new skills and meet people. Live the moment!"

Notes

Action

"Show your strength through the mirror of humility: by being confident, by being assertive, by being focused."

Notes

Action

"Don't isolate yourself too much as you could be missing on your humanity. We are stronger together."

Notes

Action

"Don't overreact when facing a new situation. Just take a step back before moving forward again."

Notes

Action

"Never limit your vision to 180°. Never limit time to now and then. Always believe in your truth."

Notes

Action

"Achieve your goal by stretching the time and space."

Notes

Action

"Give yourself space to think. Declutter your personal space."

Notes

Action

"Let the process run its course. Let the plan come to fruition. Don't doubt it, don't rush it, don't lose faith. Just let it be!"

Notes

Action

"The world is a small place. Find the location and people to achieve success. Just look up, and you will find them."

Notes

Action

"To be successful, you need to judge others with the same yardstick that you use to judge yourself."

Notes

Action

"Don't overthink life. It will happen!"

Notes

Action

"Let people be themselves; you can't change them.
Just give them the space and time to really be."

Notes

Action

"Seize the day! Take the opportunity. Trust your instinct!"

Notes

Action

"Don't rush the process. Stay focused until the end. When running, don't visualize the finish line but 10 meters beyond it!"

Notes

Action

"Create a new perspective. Change the angle. Rewire your brain. Change your rituals. Make small changes like using the hand you do things with left instead of right and vice versa."

Notes

Action

"Breathe to recover. Breathe to recharge. Breathe to
be present."

Notes

Action

"To keep on track: Focus on being present, focus on your motto, and focus beyond the finishing line."

Notes

Action

"To regenerate your strength, alertness, and power:
Sleep is the best booster."

Notes

Action

"If you don't sleep enough, exercise to compensate."

Notes

Action

"Take time to reflect! Is your environment conducive to growth? Is your lifestyle conducive to growth? Is your mindset conducive to growth? Take your time and effect the change you want!"

Notes

Action

"First, love yourself. Second, love yourself. Third, love yourself. Feel it, say it, live it!"

Notes

Action

"Have you thought about your motto? Remember, your motto will keep you on track and signpost the right way."

Notes

Action

December

"Identify boundaries that should not be crossed, by oneself or anyone wanting to join you on your journey."

Notes

Action

"Don't keep it inside; make sure people know how you feel without anger, violence, or bitterness of any kind. Just be true to yourself."

Notes

Action

"Stick to your vision. Don't be swayed by emotional influences."

Notes

Action

"Create space to grow. Declutter, clear the mess. Create time to grow; accept the silence. Create ways to grow; develop your skills."

Notes

Action

"The secret is love."

Notes

Action

"Language: Be aware that everything you say has an impact on you, others, and your environment."

Notes

Action

"Don't feel under pressure to do what others have done; that will fill you with anxiety. Do what you need to do to fulfil your potential in your own way."

Notes

Action

"I attract success and prosperity with all of my ideas."

Notes

Action

"Affirmation 2: Every thought, every word spoken, every action has an impact. I can, therefore, 'create' by first thinking, then speaking, and then doing."

Notes

Action

"Don't forget to smile in order to find that inner strength and willingness to succeed!"

Notes

Action

"Affirmation 3: Don't panic, I will find my way, I will hear my calling, I will be myself."

Notes

Action

"Affirmation 4: I believe, I can do it. I believe, I can achieve. I believe, I deserve it. I believe in me."

Notes

Action

"Affirmation 5: I keep my wits about me to avoid making major mistakes and stay on track."

Notes

Action

"Affirmation 6: I never rush as I am prepared. I never rush as I am ready. I never rush as I am calm. I embody 'serenity.'"

Notes

Action

"Affirmation 7: Open your eyes, open your heart, open your soul, and the solution of your life enigma will reveal itself."

Notes

Action

"To reach the finishing line, you need to aim past it!"

Notes

Action

"Make sure that you live the life in front of you…
every day!"

Notes

Action

"Enjoy the day fully by following your plan. But don't forget: To breathe, to rest, to smile."

Notes

Action

"Embrace this festive season and show your love to fellow human beings."

Notes

Action

"Don't take shortcuts to achieve, as you will end up on the more difficult path. Are you ready for it?"

Notes

Action

"Be rational and solution-focused, but don't forget your instinct: Let it speak, let it do, and let it guide you."

Notes

Action

"A great life booster is showing gratitude."

Notes

Action

"To find your way, you need to anchor yourself.
The thread can be physical, emotional, or spiritual."

Notes

Action

"Time will pass, but lessons need to be learnt before one can step into the next phase and carry on their path. Silence, humility, forgiveness, and love will be your tools to succeed."

Notes

Action

"Learn to say 'No' without bitterness, without doubt, without menace. Learn to say 'No' to be true to yourself."

Notes

Action

"To enhance your wellbeing, connect with people. Don't stay isolated; make it a conscious decision!"

Notes

Action

"Be mindful but not hypervigilant."

Notes

Action